Loving Someone You don't kr

Blu

Loving Someone You Don't Even Know

Zynthia Howard

Blurred Lines

This series is dedicated to all the young women who have or currently are experiencing these issues that I'm going to talk about. I wrote this for you, so that you know that there is an end to this thing, and it isn't death. There is happiness, fulfillment, and purpose right there inside of you. Chains are meant to be broken. Today is the day that they break.

Zynthia Howard

Loving Someone You don't know

Introduction ………..page 1

Finding Out Where It All Begun…..page 7

Dealing With It….page 11

Making Peace With It….page 14

Let God Take It From You.. page 17

Let Him Fill Those Voids… page 20

Embrace The Free You…page 23

Ending Prayer…page 24

Blurred Lines

Loving Someone You don't know

Have you ever thought about writing a four-page love letter to a person you've never been introduced to? Have you ever woken up early in the morning, went shopping for clothes, jewelry, and food for someone you don't have a clue what they like? Have you? Sounds silly right? The same way you are looking at these questions like: Who would do this foolishness? It's the exact way when you're trying to love yourself, yet you don't even know you. Now some people may say, how are you not going to know the person you look at every day? Before you ever go through something hurtful, traumatic, disappointing, or just some stuff that makes you feel like, "You know what, I quit", you are the authentic YOU. The real deal YOU. No doubt about it YOU. Who you can be, YOU. Can't nobody be me, like me, YOU. You see the name, YOU.

Ooh, but when you start going through some stuff. Especially in your childhood. Ooh baby, your mind gets so wrapped up, taped up, junked up, and eventually covered up. Now let me ask you this. Can you see your car keys if it's covered up by fifteen shirts and twenty-five pairs of pants? You better not lie. Now with that being said, how do you expect to be able to see you when there is a pile of hurt over here, a stack of disappointments over there, a valley of trauma slightly to the left, and if you bust that right and lean a little bit to the side, bam! Emptiness, no love, no sense of direction, chilling and eating loaded nachos with that good cheese.

There is no way you will be able to see your true self. You are covered up. Guess what? As time goes by, the stuff that's already there invites more things to ride along with you. That's right. You started out being hurt, and by the time the dust clears, baby you're hurt. Depressed, low self-esteem, don't know your worth, keep attracting people who won't treat you right, getting used by people, always crying because your emotions are all over the place. Attachment issues, suicidal, gaining and losing weight, hair falling out, can't sleep at night but you got be at work at 3a.m. Got a rash coming on your arm and don't know what it is, don't know where you fit, seems like you're always in compromising situations. You're naïve, following what seems to be making other people happy, feeling like it's a fight to make people see the diamond that you are, running in the church every Wednesday and two times on Sunday. Coming out the same and the list gets longer as you continue to carry this stuff.

As you continue to carry this stuff, these things begin to create filters over your eyes. You might be wondering, what the heck do you mean by that? Think about when it's your birthday, all day in that mode, "Hey it's my birthday, no matter what, it's going to be a lovely day!" Somebody gets smart with you, and you don't care, why? It's your birthday. It being your birthday is your filter because you are seeing your whole day by the fact that it's your birthday. Okay picture this: a woman or man is in a relationship where the other person is cheating, talking to them crazy, but they will not leave because they don't want to be lonely. Loneliness is their filter. They are basing their decision to stay because they don't want to be lonely.

You begin to look through these filters once a seed has been planted. What is a seed? A seed is an event that changes the way you feel about people and yourself. A seed is whatever happened to you at some point in your life that was hurtful, or just plain not the way things should be. Once a seed is planted, it just grows into other things over time if it's not properly dealt with. In other words, it creates more issues within you. For you to get rid of the issues you might be dealing with, you must go back and find out what the seed was. You must go back to where it all began.

Finding Out Where It All began

Finding out where it all began is an important step into finding out what seed was planted in your heart. The seed is the root of it all. The root is simply where it all started. Sometimes it is in your childhood and at other times it's in your teen or adulthood. I'm not saying this is an overnight or even a two-day process, but it's not a forever process.

For example, I had low self esteem issues for years which caused me to make poor decisions when it came to putting people in my life. I didn't just wake up with low self esteem. There was a seed planted within me at a very young age. What was the seed? When I was little, my family members would make fun of me for being hairy and then when I would go to school, kids would call me ugly all the time. They would make fun of my nose and say that made me ugly. I didn't have anyone in my life to tell me otherwise, so I started to believe it. I carried this seed into my adulthood and couldn't seem to believe that I was beautiful. I didn't really like to look in the mirror most of the time. I would often fantasize about getting a nose job. In my mind I thought that would make me look beautiful.

Just like me, you must go back in the past and discover what the seed was, and dig that thing up! I used to have trust issues. Why do you think I had trust issues? I had them because in the past people would lie and tell my most personal business to other people. That was my seed for not having trust in people.

When I separated from my ex husband, I had hate in my heart when it came to men. Now don't get it twisted, it didn't turn me off from men, but at the time I didn't care how bad I did them. Why? It was because he hurt me. The things that he did to stab me in the heart were seeds.

I used to never feel accepted around the people I would choose to have in my life. This caused me to try to act like them just to feel accepted. It caused me to try to dress like them, and wear my hair like them. Choosing to be around people who didn't really accept made me feel like there was something wrong with the way I was, and that I needed to change it. That was a seed.

I talked to a young man one day and his view was: if a man is taking care of the household and nothing is lacking, so what if he is cheating? He thought that was right because when his parents were married, his dad provided for the household, but he was a cheater. Well, the mother got tired of it and divorced him. After the divorce, their living situation wasn't the same. Their quality of life declined because they no longer had that income in the house. A seed had been planted.

Have you ever met a man or a woman who thinks everybody wants the person they're dating? They are crazy when it comes to them. I mean they will cut you! They will half way go to jail behind you even looking like you like them. I bet you were thinking that they are so insecure! Nobody wants them but them. You better believe that they did not wake up acting that way. There was a seed planted somewhere in their past to make them act like that. Most likely they probably were cheated on, or one of their close friends or family members betrayed them by sleeping with their man or woman. In their mind, that will not happen again, and if it does somebody is going to pay.

Have you ever met a person who won't give a penny to a baby? I have met a person like that. This person used to give it to everyone if they had it. The moment they found out that a person they were helping all the time was lying about needing help, they stopped helping anybody. The person lying to them about needing help was a seed that caused that person to not want to help anyone in that manner again.

Whatever issue or issues you may have. there is a seed to them all. We must be willing to discover the ugly truth about what is hidden in our heart. Sweeping it under the rug will not help you. Acting like you're over it, won't fix it either. Finding out where it all began is the only way you will be able to get rid of those issues once and for all. Once you find out the root/seed then the next step is to deal with it.

Dealing With It

What does dealing with it mean? Dealing with it, is when you can face the what. You can face what happened in your past. When you face something, you can talk about it straight up with no sugar coating. Being able to talk about how it made you feel even with that ugly crying face. You know the one. The one with the snot running out of your nose and a little bit getting in your mouth. As you are crying, the vein in your neck pops out a little bit. Yeah, that one.

Dealing with it has its benefits. You're probably thinking: what kind of benefit is there dealing with the past? Well by dealing with it, you can let the hurt out, instead of it staying in. For example, I met a woman whose mother died, and she wouldn't deal with the fact that she was dead. She didn't allow herself to go through the emotions of losing a person who was dear to her heart. In return, her health was starting to decline. She finally decided to deal with the passing of her mother. She allowed herself to grieve.

You must allow yourself to feel the emotions that were the result of what you experienced. We are not robots, nor super humans. Everybody has feelings, I don't care how tough you claim to be. If you don't allow yourself to feel those emotions, they will just be bottled up, and one day it will hit you like a cannon.

Sometimes you can't face your past by yourself. At that moment you must find safe ears. Everybody isn't equipped to walk with you as you face the past. Everybody is not built to walk with you hand and hand through the very thing that broke you spiritually, mentally, physically and emotionally. You also need to prepare yourself to be able to walk through it on your own. You must walk through it. There are no shortcuts, only cover ups. Eventually cover ups get exposed. Why is it that cover ups get exposed? It's because you can't hide what's in you. It comes out in everything you do. Its like that nagging bee on a hot summer day that will not stop flying around your head. You know the one. The bee that keeps stopping right by your ear, hanging out. That's what it's like with what's inside of you. It nags at you until you face it and get it out.

Now when you are dealing with it, you must come with a certain mindset. You must come with the intention of getting past this thing once and for all. Not just words but truly getting past it. Today society is always saying, "Keep it one hundred!" What about yourself? What about keeping it one hundred with you? Keeping it real with you is way more important than any of that other foolishness. Can you keep it real with somebody else but can't tell yourself the truth? At one point in my life I was walking around like I wasn't hurt. I was lying to myself daily. I didn't want to face that hurt. It was too painful to face. I ran from it for a little while.

 Let me tell you a secret. People can see the truth that you are hiding. They just take notes in their mind and when you mess around and make them mad, bam! They throw it up in your face to try to inflict extreme hurt. They use it as bullets to shoot you down further. Ask me how I know. Shoot out what they are wearing that is not so pretty, and they will be ready to kill you.

It's in your best interest to just face it head first. It's time to change clothes. Those old outfits stop fitting after a while. Aren't you tired of wearing those same old depressing clothes anyway? Let's deal with it.

Blurred Lines

Making Peace With It

After you have dealt with it, you then must make peace with it. Now what does making peace with it mean? It's when you get to that point of being able to let it go. This is the number one problem that people are having. They just can't seem to let it go. What keeps you in this mindset? You feel like you have the right to feel this way about the situation? Guess what? To make peace with it, you must give up that right to feel the way you do about the situation. Yes! Yes! Ladies and gents, you must give that up!

Don't you want peace within? You are not going to sit up here and tell me that feeling the way you do about the situation is peaceful. How is hating the very sight of somebody peaceful? How is feeling angry about a situation peaceful? How is it every time you hear their name, it makes you go in a rage, peaceful? How is running into anybody connected to the very thing that hurt you, make you suicidal, peaceful?

Take me for an example. I was holding all this anger inside of me pertaining to my marriage. Oh, he hurt me! I'm not talking about falling off the bike because my chain popped, kind of hurt. I'm talking about getting shot five times in the back, and stabbed in the chest, kind of hurt. I thought I had the right to be mad because he hurt the very person who really loved him. I loved him despite his flaws and he chose to hurt me. Oh, no baby, I thought I had the right to hate him forever!

I didn't have any peace. Every time he texted me, my mood immediately changed. I would go from yay to ugh! I hated his guts! I was walking in my right to hate him for the hurt he inflicted on my heart.

You want to know what walking in that right does for you? It steals your joy. Oh yes! Yes ma'am and yes sir. What kind of joy do you get when you are walking in that right? Oh, you think you have joy because you can laugh at a joke? Oh, you think you have joy because you can tell a joke? Oh, you think you have joy because you're smiling while you dance to your favorite song? Nope, that's false joy. That's surface joy. That's not joy from within. The joy from within is when you start smiling for no reason. That's the moment when you are just going about your normal routine and that smile just creeps up on you. Then. before you know it you are doing your own salsa routine throughout the house. After that you start laughing like crazy at yourself. Then you get in the shower because now you have worked up a sweat. When the water hits you, here it goes again, remix, that in the shower routine hits you. You're in the shower running all of your hot water out, haven't put not one spot of soap on you. Now that's deep joy from within.

Do you want true joy that lies deep within you? Let go of that right to feel the way you do about the situation. It doesn't matter what they have done. Let go of that right. Once you let go of that right, you are ready to truly release it. You are ready to pass it just like basketball players pass the ball on the court to that star player so he can make that 3-pointer shot to win. Who is your star player? God.

Let God Take It From You

Cast your burden on the Lord(release it) and he will sustain and uphold you. Psalms 55:22 AMP

Take your hands off of it. Come on, all five fingers. It's okay, you can trust him with it. He is the only one who can truly take every trace of it from you. He's like the bounty paper towel commercials. I'm sure you've seen it. When the kid wastes red juice all over the counter and the bounty paper towels soak up every trace of red juice. It's like the spill never happened. That's how God will take that from you. I know it sounds cliché and unbelievable, but trust him and see what happens. I double dare you to pass that very thing that broke you to him.

Have you ever known somebody who's been through all kinds of stuff? They've experienced losing kids, money, places to lay their head, and they're steady going through things. Yet you see them, and it's like none of those things never happened to them. You know why? They have passed all those things to God and he truly took it. He took that burden of them having to deal with the hurt and frustration that came from those situations.

God is just waiting with his arms wide to take all those things from you completely. He doesn't partially do anything. He does it all the way. It's like when you're at burger king and you order a whopper. What do they ask you? "You want that made all the way?" What do you say in return? "Yes, put everything on there!" He is not a half stepper.

He will take it all from you. He is a gentleman. He will not make you give it to him. It's your choice. Choose to let him take it. He's not like anybody you've ever met. Sometimes we don't want to dump our problems on people because we feel like it's unfair to them, and they probably don't want to hear it. He is not like that. He wants to hear all about it. Guess what? When you're done talking all about it, he wants to keep it. You don't ever have to worry about dealing with it ever again. It's like when a person has been getting bullied at school everyday until they finally open their mouth and tell their big brother. You know the one. He lives and breathes at the gym. He benches four hundred on his worst day.

He goes to the school to have a talk with the bully, and the problem is solved. No more problems. God is like your big brother. Once you give it to him, the problem is solved. He takes the burden from you right then. He moves immediately.

After he takes it, that thing that you were carrying all those years no longer becomes a secret anymore. Your shoulders get lighter. Sometimes you might even lose weight. I know you're like, 'what?' Yes! You don't realize while you are carrying those burdens, that they are having major effects on your body. It's like a person who was totally healthy, but when they lose a loved one, they die a few months later. Grief took over and started to affect the body entirely. That person didn't give that grief to God. We are no match for the burdens that we carry. We will lose every time if we continue to try to carry them.

You don't have to let those things that you are carrying take over you and ultimately kill you. They can kill you physically, mentally, emotionally, and spiritually. Have you ever seen a person who goes to sleep angry, and wakes up the same way? They have a permanent frown on their face like a tattoo. Do you want to be like that? Let him have it. This is what the phrase "let it go and let God have it" means. Let it go, and let God have it.

Let Him Fill Those Voids

My Soul(my life, my inner self) thirst for God, for the living God; Psalms 42:2 AMP

Now that you have given it to him, there are voids where those burdens that you used to carry lived. Voids are like holes in the wall of your house. Now we both know what happens when you have a hole in your house. Rats, spiders, cats, dogs, lizards, squirrels and whatever else decides to come in will be in your house. What would you do to keep those things out if you had holes in your wall? You will fill in those holes and seal them up.

You are the house and now have holes in your house. Trust and believe that there are some things that want to fill those holes in your house. As a matter of fact. those things you gave to God would like to come back with vengeance. How do you fill

Loving Someone You Don't Know

those holes and seal them off? You fill those holes with God. How do you do that? You take in everything he has to say about you. You make him your bestie. You make him your ride or die. You race home everyday to tell him all about your day. You tell him your ideas and ambitions. Let him in every area of your life, don't leave anything out. Even the smallest things, like how to wear your hair. Don't you know he is concerned about even the smallest things that have to do with you? He will never get tired of you talking. Give him special time to spend with you. All you need is time to just bask in his presence. How do you get in his presence? Invite him in. Tell him how you appreciate him. Tell him how much you love him. Love on him. He likes to be loved just like the rest of us, you know.

Then you go to his word. As you read, he will reveal to you what everything you are reading means. As you do this every day, he fills all those voids and seals them up. He seals them up with that good stuff. What he seals it up with is better than crazy glue. It's stronger than storm doors and the finest steel.

Blurred Lines

It's like when you have surgery, and your body heals from the wound. At first you felt awful right after the surgery, but when it healed you felt like a million bucks. This is how you are going to feel when he fills those voids with him. You will feel like a different person. You will have to learn how to function all over again. This will be a place you have never been before. A place of freedom that you have never experienced. It's like when a person has been locked up for thirty years, and they get released from prison and back into society. They don't know how to act at all because they've been locked up for so long. Now that they're free, they must adjust to being free. They don't have those boundaries that they once faced in prison.

You will feel this way. It's okay because if you let God lead you, he will begin to show you the correct way to function. He will give you new habits to practice. He will change your entire mindset. You won't be able to think the same even if you want to.

You will look in the mirror, and won't even recognize yourself. That's how much you will change. It will show in your appearance. Have you ever seen someone really going through something, and when it's over it looks like their skin is glowing? It's because that burden is gone. Burdens don't shine on you. They take the light away from you.

Embrace The Free You

Before I formed you in the womb I knew you(and approved of you as my chosen instrument); Jeremiah 1:5 AMP

Have you ever thought about getting reintroduced to yourself? Let me tell you, I never did. I thought I knew myself. No need for an introduction. I was in for a rude awakening. I was covered up with so much stuff, I didn't have a clue. When I got free, God introduced me to myself. He began to show me who I was. I'm not pulling your leg, or telling some false story. This is real talk, a true story.

He reminded me of skills that I forgot I even had. Now I know what you're probably thinking. How

Loving Someone You Don't Know

can you forget a natural born skill? I'm telling you, it can get buried with all the mess that's on you. I had forgotten that I could draw, write poetry, sing, and that I love to write and tell stories. He began to show me that again.

One day while I was washing my face, he stopped me and began to show me the beauty in my face. I was like wow, I have not been able to see this in years. I just stood and looked at myself in awe, like this is me.

He literally introduced me to me. He was like 'Zynthia, meet the person that I created from birth.' You know, sometimes you spend a good bit of your life trying to be someone you were never created to be. That was me. Somewhere in my life I got so covered up that it buried the real me alive. When I got free! Uh oh, here she comes! It's like when you're at a football game, and those cheerleaders are on the sidelines cheering the players on for the win. This is how God is when it comes to embracing your freedom. He walks beside you everyday, pushing you to walk in everything that makes you the person that he created.

Blurred Lines

As people try to get in your ear, he will shut them down with no, no, I said you are x,y,z. Trust me, you will never walk in anyone else's shoes. You will only drive in your lane. He will make sure of it.

As you begin to embrace your freedom, you will further get to know him on a deeper level. You will go to a place where you have never been. He will show you things about yourself you never could imagine. He knows you better than anybody you will ever meet.

Whatever he says about you is the truth and nothing else. Don't even waste your time trying to debate it. It's undebatable without a doubt. You will not only develop a deep love for him, but for yourself as well. This love is a different kind of love. This love runs deep. It's unshakeable. It's an "I know you're lying", kind of love. You think you feel free when it's Friday and you're off for the weekend. No, no honey! It's better than that kind of freedom. This is a permanent freedom that never gets erased. There is no more clocking back into the things that held you down.

Can you imagine waking up with nothing on your mind? Can you imagine going to sleep at a decent time? When you are burdened down, sleep is a figment of your imagination. I used to go to sleep everywhere! Honey I used to go to sleep in the club, restaurants, standing up, sometimes driving. Why? I couldn't sleep at night because I was burdened down. I was getting tormented by it. I would wake up feeling like somebody kicked me fifty times in the back. Baby, now as soon as it looks like it's getting dark, I'm on my way to sleep. When I wake up, I feel so refreshed. I put my reggae gospel music on. and 'pon de way' to the kitchen.

I have a peace that I have never experienced. I have a peace that I didn't even know existed. That ex husband I mentioned earlier? I can talk to him with no anger in my heart. God took it from me. I don't even think about it anymore. The only thing I think about now is who I am. Yes! I know who I am now. I'm no longer lost. I no longer need anyone to validate me. I have the ultimate validation. The validation from God. I love me. I love the *real* me! I love every part of my reflection. I'm free!

You can be free too! It's not just for me. It's available to you too. Come on here, and get your freedom! This is a party that doesn't stop. You don't have to wait until your birthday, holiday, or a family gathering. God is the ultimate DJ. The way your life will spin will be beyond what you could ever imagine.

Ending Prayer

Lord, forgive us for we have sinned and repent of our sins, known and unknown to

Loving Someone You Don't Know

us. We thank you for who you are, we thank you for being everything to us, we thank you for all the things that you have done. Things that you are doing and for the things that you are about to do. We come against hurt, disappointment, shame, abuse, anger, malice, word curses, damnation, any hindrances, violations, grief, low self-esteem, identity crisis, insomnia, confusion, vengeance, strife, combativeness, control, negative thinking, offense. I command them to go in the name of Jesus. I release the love of God, freedom and peace upon your mind, body and your spirit in Jesus name.

Visit my Zynthia Howard poetry page on Facebook for daily inspirational poetry.

Blurred Lines

Made in the USA
Columbia, SC
06 March 2024